CONDITIONING
Your Soul

NEIL B. WISEMAN

Beacon Hill Press of Kansas City
Kansas City, Missouri

Library of Congress Cataloging-in-Publication Data

Wiseman, Neil B.
    Conditioning your soul / Neil B. Wiseman.
      p.   cm. — (Pastoral quick read series)
    Includes bibliographical references.
    ISBN 0-8341-1767-3 (pbk.)
    1. Clergy—Religious life. I. Title. II. Series.
    BV4011.6.W57   1999
    248.8'92—dc21

                             99-32626
                             CIP

10 9 8 7 6 5 4 3 2 1

Contents

Soul Conditioning for Leaders

Spiritual fitness is essential for every leader in the Body of Christ. Vigorous, regular soul conditioning is as imperative for a Christian leader as physical exercise is essential for a star athlete.

Even though physical exercise may be excruciating or inconvenient, it improves endurance and flexibility, lowers tension and fatigue, and reduces injuries even as it provides resistance to disease. Exercise even increases energy. What a desirable list of benefits.

Amazingly, we reap similar benefits when we develop our inner life. When we condition our soul, we experience improved endurance, energy, and flexibility even as it lowers tension and reduces fatigue. Spiritual conditioning reduces danger of injury and improves resistance to germs and viruses.

Soul conditioning empowers leaders. Exercising the soul enables leaders to meet demands that test their limits. One over-stressed minister understood the pressures when he remarked, "Ministry sometimes feels like being chased by an unfriendly

Doberman." In our time, ministry frequently feels like the emotional equivalent of an automobile accident, a war, a crashing jet, a flood tide on the Mississippi, and a 500-mile hurricane rolled together.

Obviously, then, being a Kingdom leader requires more than excellent training or highly experienced competency. The incredible demands of contemporary ministry highlight both the problem and possibility.

Neglecting personal spiritual fitness is one of our most common problems. Frederick Buechner is accurate when he warns, "Ministers are famous for neglecting their selves with the result that they are apt to become in their own way as hopeless and crippled as the people they are trying to care for and thus no longer selves who can be of much help to others" (*Listening to Your Life* [San Francisco: Harper San Francisco, 1992], 320). A leader who neglects himself becomes like a football player with a broken shoulder, a heart surgeon with a broken hand, or a lawyer with a confused memory. Buechner uses two clever sentences to summarize this need: "'Mind your own business' means butt out of other people's lives . . . but it also means pay attention to your own life, your own health and wholeness, both for your own sake and ultimately for the sake of those you lead. Take care of yourself so you can take care of them" (Buechner, 320-21).

Another amazing possibility is also present. The God who comes alongside strengthens us as we commit to personal spiritual fitness. Ministry done in mere human strength never accomplishes much. But, when human weakness is divinely enabled, it overcomes every obstacle. Supernatural strength comes to us through our strong Savior when we cultivate our inner spiritual life.

Alan Jones, the California Anglican priest, clarifies the issue: "Leaders need to be so committed to their own spiritual journeys, and the truth telling it involves, that they can learn to be centered and still be in the middle of raging storms" (*Sacrifice and Delight* [San Francisco: Harper Collins, 1992], 50). Ministry centered on the Master can withstand any frustration or storm.

The good news is that a sturdy soul is strong enough to see us through. Sufficient for every test, this conditioning strengthens soul stamina and builds moral muscle. You can count on it. Every effort of spiritual formation increases energy, endurance, strength, and flexibility.

The significance of soul conditioning is delightfully affirmed by a story told by William Barclay. A busy Glasgow pastor told of attending a service conducted by a minister preacher who had occupied an influential pulpit for long years, written several books, effectively accomplished the work of a city shepherd, and represented the cause of Christ in civic affairs. The visiting pastor said to the other minister, "Sir, when I think of the strain of preaching from this influential pulpit, I do not know how you have carried on all these years." The other minister answered quietly, "In this work, you do not carry on; you are carried on."

We, too, are "carried on" when we apply God's promises to the details of our days:

"Cast your burden on the Lord, and he will sustain you" (Ps. 55:22).

"When you pass through the waters I

will be with you; and through the rivers, they shall not overwhelm you" (Isa. 43:2).

"The eternal God is your dwelling place, and underneath are the everlasting arms" (Deut. 33:27).

Your whole spiritual weight can rest on this well-demonstrated reality. God will sustain you beyond the breaking point and keep you from breaking. Soul conditioning makes leaders able to victoriously face anything. Undergirding our education, skill, and acceptance, we still have Christ, and that's enough—extravagantly enough.

Meanwhile, a surprising serendipity happens to us. As we grow spiritually, we know better how to help others grow. We realize teaching someone else to grow a sturdy soul can be complicated, confusing work. In fact, it is almost impossible until we master the art ourselves. But as our own spiritual conditioning strengthens us, we are better prepared to know how to help others grow. So everyone gains when a leader seriously works at growing a sturdy soul.

I receive special inspiration from evangelist Vance Havner's insights about min-

CONDITIONING

istry, "We develop health of the soul as of the body by daily programs of rest, diet, exercise. And happy is the minister who has gained vigor of soul and can go about helping the soul-sick of earth find the health he enjoys" (*In Tune with Heaven* [Baker, 1990], 28). What an adventure to develop healthy souls so we can be soul physicians to those entrusted to our care. The secret of soul health is a consuming commitment to know Christ better every day of ministry.

But how does a leader initiate and maintain spiritual fitness in the midst of a crowded life and busy ministry? How does one keep focused on Christ rather than chaos, on hope rather than despair, and on opportunities rather than obstacles?

Let's consider 20 suggestions. Perhaps some of these will help you grow a sturdy soul.

1. COMMIT TO PERSONAL SOUL CARE.

To make time for spiritual fitness, a leader must control priorities, unreasonable demands, and secular values. Self-care deserves high priority because it is the driving force for everything a leader does.

Like persons in other walks of life, pastors desire a life that produces meaning and purpose. Such a quality life comes from a Christ-saturated way of living centered on our Lord's teachings, energized by His closeness, and steeped in His will. This means a leader's responsibilities must make room for the absolute essential of cultivating a God-shaped life and then sharing that quality life with others.

To nourish such a quality life, a Christian leader must remember he or she is a consumer of grace, not its creator. The leader is merely one of God's channels of grace to others.

To faithfully care for his or her soul, a leader must learn to use reading, praying, and knowing God. These are gushing springs that refresh the soul. These resources are powerfully connected in this quote from New Testament scholar William Barclay, "Every time we pray, 'Our Father,' we can know for certain that for God no one is lost in the crowd; that if we matter to no one else, we matter to God; that if no one else cares for us, God cares. That's something to lift up our hearts every time we pray" (Ronald Barclay, ed., *Daily Reading with William Barclay* [San Francisco: Harper San Francisco, 1992], 20).

Self-care connected like a lifeline to Jesus deepens devotion to the Lord and helps an individual demonstrate Christlikeness in every cranny and corner of life.

The minister's personal commitment to soul conditioning sometimes ignites a whole congregation with holy zeal. Then church members, served by a spiritually growing leader, begin to feel a need to grow themselves. They are drawn to spiritual development when they see a leader's spiritual self-care showing in noble moments, catastrophes, victories, and ambiguities.

Sadly, without vibrant spiritual self-care, a pastor usually sentences himself to leading a religious business, a do-good relief agency, or an affable social club. Any of those produce a boring life.

Moses offered us insightful advice, "Take heed to thyself, and keep thy soul diligently, lest thou forget the things which thine eyes have seen, and lest they depart from thy heart all the days of thy life" (Deut. 4:9, KJV).

Spiritual Exercises

1. Take your day-by-day appoint-ment calendar and reserve one-half day per week to care for your soul.
2. Make a list of ways to nourish your devotion to Christ.
3. Mark a date on your calendar af-ter four weeks to evaluate your progress.

THE MINISTER'S
PERSONAL
COMMITMENT TO
SOUL CONDITIONING
SOMETIMES IGNITES
A WHOLE
CONGREGATION WITH
HOLY ZEAL.

2. CHERISH SIMPLE ABUNDANCE.

The term "simple abundance" comes from Sarah Ban Breathnach's best-selling book. Though it is doubtful the author intended for it to be a Christian book, *Simple Abundance* touches a raw nerve with a call to balance spiritual longings with overwhelming and conflicting commitment at home, work, church, and in the community. A powerful sentence from the book's foreword summarizes the issue: "I wanted so much—money, success, recognition, genuine creative expression—but had absolutely no clue as to what I truly needed" (*Simple Abundance* [New York: Warner Books, 1995], foreword).

Wants and needs keep confusing us across our lifetime.

How does the simple abundance idea apply to a church leader? Because they have high visibility and because they desire to be of maximum use to the Kingdom, leaders can find themselves almost unconsciously seeking status and prominence. Alan Jones warns, "The appetite for personal influence can be all-consuming, especially when we tell ourselves that it is to help others" (52).

You can keep secular poisons from shrinking your soul. At the same time you can enrich your life by using the simple abundance idea. Here are ways to do it.

✳ Count your blessings rather than fretting about problems. Face it, everyone you meet has at least one problem. And everyone has some blessings. The songwriter offers glorious advice, "Count your many blessings / . . . and it will surprise you what the Lord hath done."

Though every human being has some misery in life, every difficulty can be overcome through Christ's victory that is at work in us.

✳ Value perks. You would not have your present assignment if someone did not believe in you. Someone thinks you are worthy of support. Someone loves you for your work's sake. Someone counts on you to be strong and noble and loving. Like wildflowers in the Rockies, beautiful and unique perks surround ministry leaders in rich profusion all along the pilgrimage of ministry.

In *Heart of a Great Pastor,* H. B. London

and I wrote, "Thousands of memories flood my mind when I reflect on the essence of ministry. I think of incredible perks I have received while representing Christ. I intend to stay in ministry all my life so I can continue enjoying these amazing surprises and incredible fringe benefits."

Later in the same book, I commented on perks: "I love the privilege of living at the front lines of life where grace works and where the peace treaties of reconciliation are co-signed by God and broken people. As flawed and frail as I know myself to be, I am privileged to represent Christ at the main events of people's lives" (H. B. London and Neil B. Wiseman, *Heart of a Great Pastor* [Ventura, Calif.: Regal Books, 1994], 135).

To see what grace does in the lives of those we serve is a simple abundance of the ministry. What a magnificent perk for a leader to remember that ministry is a thousand times more important than ticker-tape parades or monuments in our honor.

❋ **Commit to what really counts.** Increasingly, contemporary pastors are ordering their lives by a realization that more members, more staff, more buildings, more money, and more benefits are not the central issues in our service for Christ. Instead, leaders seem to be rediscovering what they always knew—eternal issues revolve around transformed people who find Jesus and order their lives by His teachings.

Recognize the satisfactions of simple abundance. Find unspeakable joy in serving people. Rejoice that you are a spiritual midwife to new converts. Multiply your satisfactions by concentrating on what matters. Ignore trivia and invest in what counts for eternity.

✳ **Make your marriage great.** Many single persons are involved in ministry, and their work deserves honor. But marriage is a splendid gift you give yourself as well as your spouse. Develop your marriage across a lifetime as an investment that pays daily. Cherish and cultivate the simple abundance found in a Christ-centered creative marriage.

We live in a world of ministry where we have many simple abundances to enjoy.

Our challenge is to inventory the simple riches we already have all around us. Consider how much you have of what really matters. Much of what we take for granted stands waiting to bless our thoughts, memories, and perspectives.

Make Sarah Breathnach's advice work in your life: "Let's choose today to quench our thirst for the 'good life' we think others lead by acknowledging the good that already exists in our own lives" (*Simple Abundance,* January 6).

Are you ready to try? Thank God for your spouse, children, and/or extended family. Drive by your church. Think of all who welcome you into their lives for ministry and friendship. The results from taking such an inventory of your simple abundances will stretch your soul and make you sing. Every Christian leader, even those with disappointments and pain, is surrounded by simple abundances he or she seldom thinks to consider.

Even in simple things, God is graciously good.

LEARN TO LOVE

THOSE YOU LEAD,

WARTS AND ALL.

3. LEARN TO LOVE PEOPLE.

If a pastor and congregation do not love each other, the church suffers. Sadly, many ministers keep their people at arm's length. Then parishioners feel distant from a leader and a leader feels isolated in a crowd. The spiritual health of a church and its leader requires more than religious professionalism. Check 1 Cor. 13 for delightful discovery.

God means for every church to be a holy family and for every minister to be the spiritual head of that family. Learn to love those you lead, warts and all. Loving imperfect people is nothing new. It's a fact of life that most of those we serve are not perfect. Affirming and affectionate relational ties attract people to any church and at the same time bring lasting satisfaction to the leader.

Before a surprised world and the critical gaze of tradition religionists, Christ demonstrated that love is more essential than efficient organizational charts, orderly parliamentary procedures, or strategies we sometimes borrow from secular society.

Spiritual Exercises

Make a list of simple abundances
that enrich your life. Star items
unique to your life.

1.

2.

3.

4.

5.

6.

7.

8.

9.

10.

23

Pastoral Quick Read Series

4. USE CONVENIENT RESOURCES.

To ripen your soul, view the multiplicities of ministry as gigantic opportunities for your own spiritual growth. Raw materials are everywhere around you.

As a beginning point, view personal soul development as more than religious veneer for public display. Realize that spiritual maturity does not come by spontaneous osmosis. Handling holy things and sharing biblical ideas do not make anyone spiritual. Leading worship services and even preaching highly energized sermons do not make us Christlike. Neither can spiritual development be caught like a flu virus from a mate, a mentor, or a member of the church. Living near the fire is good, but not good enough.

Leaders must discover raw materials from nearby gold mines. Even the busiest pastor handles spiritual dynamite many times every day. Teaching and preaching frequently take pastors to the Book of God —the oxygen line of spiritual wellness. In their daily work, ministers often pray and sometimes see miraculous results. Counseling and pastoral care take ministers to the place where the gospel transforms lives, heals broken homes, and makes faith real in the details of human existence.

Every pastor has the joy of sometimes seeing congregants live out the Christian life. Often laity take their spiritual leader at his word by applying faith to life. Their new discoveries of knowing God better can bless your own soul. Watch carefully for this reality. What you see will provide you with spiritual stamina for your own spiritual development.

The challenge, then, for a Christian leader is to make full use of nearby resources to help him or her draw closer to God.

When you pray for others, ask yourself, "What does God want me to hear?" Each time you preach, consider how God wants this truth you share to shape you. View every expression of ministry as an opportunity for personal growth. In the process, ministry will turn into a spiritual gold mine for enriching your life.

Spiritual Exercises

Evaluate and react to these statements:

1. I use preparation for preaching as a source to feed my soul.
2. I consider spiritually mature people as living commentaries for spiritual development.
3. I frequently think about ways to improve my intimacy with God.
4. I have devotional books I have never finished reading.
5. I talk with seasoned church leaders about how to be more Christlike.
6. I see spiritual growth in my people and use that awareness to enrich my own spiritual development.
7. I frequently ask God to shape my spiritual pilgrimage with my frustrations.

5. CELEBRATE YOUR CALLING AS MORE THAN A PROFESSION.

For decades, our society viewed pastors as bumbling and harmless. Even though ministers were respected, most were not taken seriously. Though this attitude continues in some places, it has radically changed in others. In many current settings, pastors are now viewed as professionals, like doctors, lawyers, social workers, and teachers.

Everyone can rejoice that contemporary Christian leaders are usually well-trained, competent, and professionally credentialed. Many drive late-model cars, wear nice clothes, and have an impressive education. While all of this sounds like a splendid improvement, the danger is that church leaders will become more committed to being persons of respect in the community than all-out disciples of the Lord Christ.

Somewhere I read that some pastors are so concerned about career development that when approached about a new assignment, the first thing that comes to their mind is the four P's: 1) pay, 2) parsonage, 3) prominence of pulpit, and 4) pensions benefits.

Though these issues are legitimate concerns they cannot become ultimate factors. Our calling as pastors means we must start with obedience and service questions. Is this where God wants me? That's the lifelong satisfaction of living out a calling.

To develop a healthy soul, a pastor must personally use the abounding resources of prayer, promises of Scripture, and the spiritual disciplines. The sturdy spiritual leader must cultivate a warm faith. He must demonstrate forgiveness and love righteousness. His compassion must be responsive and generous. And his whole ministry must be kept under loving obedience to the One who called. That's a richer way to live than any amount of professionalization could ever provide.

By overly professionalizing ministry, a leader can impoverish himself or herself and the congregation. Let's find acceptable middle ground by behaving like professionals while trusting God like dependent servants—which we are.

Case Study

Pastor Sid Morgan feels threatened whenever the relationship between call and profession is discussed. While he has no desire to be overly concerned about appearance, status, and credentials, he thinks these things really matter.

His goal is to fulfill his calling in a professional manner. He worries about being an authentic servant leader. Meanwhile, he feels embarrassed by the poor work habits and the sloppy physical appearance of some of his colleagues.

How can Sid find middle ground?

What problems occur when ministry becomes too professional?

Can a minister overemphasize a call to ministry?

| Self-Check
✓ | ***Bible Check Point*** |

Creatively interrupt your reading of this book by spending five minutes thinking about the application of the following passage to your life and ministry:

"I'm staying alert and in top condition. I'm not going to get caught napping, telling everyone else all about it and then missing out myself."

—1 Cor. 9:19, TM

✳ What does the passage say to you personally?

✳ What would it take to move you spiritually from where you are to top condition?

6. APPLY YOUR PREACHING TO YOURSELF.

Try viewing your preaching through medical lenses. A medical degree, a license to practice medicine, a thorough knowledge of pharmacology, and years of surgical experience do not keep a physician personally healthy. Obviously, doctors can practice medicine without being healthy. But to be truly healthy, doctors must live by the rules of good health they prescribe for their patients or they will become as sick as their patients.

Consider the obvious parallels between a medical doctor and a Kingdom leader. To keep spiritually well, the leader must give careful attention to inner health. This requires applying remedies to himself or herself that he or she prescribes for others.

Moses provides a biblical example for this part of our soul conditioning. In Exodus 34:29-35 we find him speaking with God face-to-face, as friend to friend. When Moses came back after the meeting with God, his face was radiant. Wouldn't you like to have a holy radiance about your person as you speak for God in preaching? David Day, the British preacher, summarizes this issue so well, "The shining face cannot be faked or kept in a jar by the study door. Moses' face shone because he had spent time in the presence of God and because God had spoken to him 'as a man speaks with his friend' . . . There is nothing more important than climbing the mountain and listening in silence" (David Day, *A Preaching Workbook* [London: LYNX Publisher, 1998], 37).

One incredibly impacting way to implement this idea is to preach from soul-stretching biblical passages. Like mountain climbing in physical conditioning, the peaks of Scripture leave us out of breath with their demands even as they inspire us with their promises and attract us with their beauty.

Preach soul-stretching themes from lofty passages. Then your own soul can grow and flourish even as your congregants draw closer to God. Check out these amazing provisions from Scripture: Exod. 19:4; Ps. 16:11; 107:20; Isa. 26:3; 45:22; Jer. 29:13; Luke 15:20; Rom. 10:13; 12:21; 2 Cor. 6:2; Rev. 21:5. Put your trust in every one of them.

CRY THE

GOSPEL

WITH YOUR

WHOLE LIFE.

7. RETAIN INTIMACY WITH GOD.

Longtime pastor Eugene H. Peterson, an authentic witness of the pastoral scene, shares this observation:

> Three pastoral acts—praying, reading Scripture, and giving spiritual direction—are so basic, so critical, that they determine the shape of everything else in ministry. Besides being basic, these three acts are quiet and done mostly out of the spotlight. Since they do not call attention to themselves, they are so often neglected. . . . Since almost never does anyone notice whether we do these things, and only occasionally does someone ask that we do them, these real acts of ministry suffer widespread neglect.

> When any of these pastoral acts— praying, reading Scripture, or giving spiritual direction—are neglected, the minister and congregation become spiritually shortchanged (*Eugene H. Peterson*, Working the Angles *[Grand Rapids: Eerdmans, 1987], 2).*

Then Peterson sounds this warning: "It

doesn't take many years in the pastorate to realize that we can conduct a fairly respectable ministry without giving much more than ceremonial attention to God. Since we can omit these acts without anybody noticing, and because each of the acts involves a great deal of rigor, it is easy and common to slight them" (3).

He is right. Vitality leaks out of ministry when a leader allows personal spirituality to become ceremonial. Then contemporary church leadership becomes more like running an organization than being a key player in the soul-saving arena of eternal redemption.

Spiritual fitness for a pastor, like everyone else, requires frequent, fresh encounters with God. Established routines are important. But don't neglect freshness. Our challenge is to approach soul development with a spirit of expectancy. Use creativity, imagination, spontaneity, delight, and even fascination to infuse meaning into habitual routines. Without freshness, spiritual vigor and ministry stamina burn low or go out altogether.

To retain spiritual freshness, we must hang out with God. Draw near Him and listen carefully. Freshness means elevating faith conditioning to a level of delightful discovery. This God-closeness, like falling in love, creates attentiveness, togetherness, and warmth. Developing intimacy with God opens our eyes to appreciate the amazing mysteries of grace and fuels fulfillment through a lifetime of ministry.

Pastor Tom Foreman called this Christ connection "a God-permeated life." What a word picture that is. The ingredients of a God-permeated life are devotion to Scripture, intimacy in prayer, and friendship with holy men and women of God who walk across the inspiring pages of devotional literature. A Christ-connected leader also esteems common, ordinary folks who do heroic service for God in out-of-the way settings; God's quiet people can teach us a lot.

All these efforts to keep spiritually fit activate Christ's extravagant promise, "Blessed are those who hunger and thirst for righteousness, *for they shall be satisfied*" (Matt. 5:6, emphasis added). That promise includes every pastor and lay leader in every church.

Spiritual Exercises

React to Eugene Peterson's sentence: "Three pastoral acts—praying, reading Scripture, and giving spiritual direction—are so basic, so critical, that they determine the shape of everything else in ministry."

If you fully accepted this statement, how would your ministry change?

How does spiritual direction affect the pastoral care, counseling, and adminstrative requirements of pastoral ministry?

Case Study—
Lessons on Guidance

Confused about administrative matters in his church, Tom Cashman sought answers from various sources. Almost as an afterthought, he checked biblical references regarding guidance, direction, and providence. Then he prayed, "Lord, this is Your church, and we want Your direction." Soon he set aside time at the beginning of decision meetings to seek guidance. As might be expected, an outspoken businessman thought they were wasting time.

However, Tom discovered God is ready to offer guidance on matters of vision and administrative issues. Tom wants to place greater emphasis on guidance in his church. Where does he start?

**SEEKING GUIDANCE
HELPS A LEADER
UNDERSTAND
GOD'S PURPOSE
FOR A SPECIFIC
CHURCH AT A
PARTICULAR TIME.**

8. PURPOSEFULLY SEEK DIRECTION FOR MINISTRY.

A minister may receive guidance for pastoral care and church administrative leadership just as he or she receives inspiration for preaching. Though pastors are experienced at waiting before God for direction for preaching, why not seek guidance for administration and clarity for mission as well?

Seeking guidance helps a leader understand God's purpose for a specific church at a particular time. The key question when seeking divine guidance must be, "What does God want for this congregation right now?" Such seeking often supplies a surprising serendipity of helping a pastor know exactly how to share vision with the congregation.

Pastor Sam Troyer explains his own experience: "When I keep close to Christ in Scripture reading and intercession, I sometimes experience a pastoral guidance system, something like radar. Then, I am aware of what Christ wants done. In trying to find God's guidance, I miss directives often enough that I do not blame Him when my impressions are inaccurate. At the other end of the spectrum, however, I have been guided often enough that I am always open to His leadership."

Another minister describes his similar experience: "Sometimes when I pray, read Scripture and listen carefully, I get assignments for First Church. Those prayer conversations invigorate me and direct my ministry. I delight to receive direction from my Commander-in-Chief during scriptural study and prayer. This is a glorious strength to me."

Seeking God in the details makes us more aware of the availability of holy guidance and assures us we are not alone.

Scripture reassures us that God is ready to guide us in every phase of our lives, including the ministry. I love this good word from the prophet Isaiah: "Whether you turn to the right or to the left, your ears will hear a voice behind you, saying, 'This is the way; walk in it'" (Isa. 30:21, NIV).

Spiritual Exercises

Review and discuss with a colleague:

1. Seeking guidance for administrative issues is common for most churches.

   ___ Agree   ___ Disagree

2. Divine guidance clarifies mission.

   ___ Agree   ___ Disagree

3. The key guidance question is: "What does God want for this congregation?"

   ___ Agree   ___ Disagree

4. Seeking guidance would save many misunderstandings.

   ___ Agree   ___ Disagree

5. The promise "I will guide you into all truth" applies to administrative decisions as well as preaching.

   ___ Agree   ___ Disagree

Case Study—
Who Can You Trust
to Be a Soul Friend?

At a theological college in Trinidad, I suggested every church leader needs a soul friend for accountability and affirmation. An alert pastor asked, "Where can such a friend be found when we have such competition among church leaders?" His question applies everywhere. How can we get started? Here's a starter list:

1. Add accountability to an existing friendship.

2. Volunteer to be a soul friend; the other person may return the favor.

3. Seek accountable friendship with more than one person—one for accountability, one for affirmation, and one to test reality.

Without a soul friend, pastors are often less effective than they could be with one.

9. CULTIVATE A SOUL FRIEND.

Every pastor needs at least one absolutely trustworthy friend to whom he or she voluntarily makes himself or herself spiritually accountable and with whom he or she can be totally candid. Ideally, a soul friend should be encouraged to question us about three critical issues—motives, marriage, and ministry.

The Christian leader must give a soul friend permission to ask hard questions about his or her relationship with God and inquire about personal purity and ministry commitments. This permission may be difficult to give anyone because so many leaders work so hard to build their image. As a result, they do not recognize their faults or would not admit them if they did. One pastor said, "I don't want anyone asking me hard questions because I don't want to know my flaws. This soul mate business makes me feel like I'm facing a spiritual firing squad."

Sadly, a failure to correct flaws eventually makes a leader weak, shallow, and nearsighted. At a time when youth are shouting,

"Get real." some church leaders are allowing themselves to become less authentic.

What kind of a person should you choose as a soul friend? It should be someone of the same gender. It may be a mentor, a colleague, a neighboring pastor, a retired minister, or a peer outside your own denomination. This friend should be one who loves you enough to be both tender and tough. Ideally, a soul friend must be willing to listen redemptively to hurts, affirm strengths, and insist upon integrity. The soul friend must always be ready to pat a pastor on the back and to question phoniness. Authentic accountability is the issue.

In seeking a soul friend, you may wish to consider two significant questions: (1) Will there be competition between us? (2) Can I trust this person with my private thoughts?

Three most critical issues:

* motives
* marriage
* ministry

A Risky Prayer for Pioneers

Father God, You often call servants to take the gospel where traditionalists were afraid to take it.

But we are ready to go where You want us to go.

We are ready to follow orders.

We want to be effective pioneers for You.

Help us to see more than we have seen.

Save us from stupidity and calling it sacrifice.

Protect us from dry rot, trifles, boredom, and rust.

Equip us for the front lines and send us on a mission worthy of Your name.

In the strong name of Jesus. Amen.

HUMANLY,

WE FEEL SECURE

HOLDING ON

TO WHAT

WE HAVE.

10. PIONEER NEW FRONTIERS.

Keeping everything the same concerning schedule, programming, music, evangelism, fund-raising, and personal spiritual development may sound attractive. But as sure as gravity, progress requires change and change creates discomfort or conflict for someone. In fact, one social scientist said change is constant; the only issue open for us to decide is whether we manage it or resist it.

Face this fact squarely—no progress is possible without change. It is also true for individuals—no change means no interior development

It is simply not possible to keep things the same because people and churches keep outgrowing their past over and over again. Humanly, we feel secure holding on to what we have. But Kingdom advances, by human standards, almost always seem risky. Check Scripture and church history for the evidence.

The precondition for achievement is change on someone's part.

A highly placed church leader from a past era liked to inquire about recruits, "Is he or she safe?" He asked about proposed programs or proposals, "Will this idea rock the boat or cause controversy?" In the process, he routinely bypassed concepts that sounded controversial. He seldom considered progressive ministers for key assignments because they were too threatening. That leader bears responsibility for serious blight to the Kingdom because he missed the energy, creative ideas, and innovation that so-called unsafe people bring to the church.

By calling for resistance to safety, I don't mean that a leader should champion stupidity, presumption, or maverick innovation for its own sake. One enthusiastic preacher thoroughly understood the issue when he advised, "Get out on the limb, that's where the best fruit is."

It is frighteningly easy for a leader to choose safety rather than move to the cutting edge of ministry. It is easier to be cautious and predictable—words that don't fit well next to God's big words, such as *gospel, mission,* and *worldwide impact.*

Here's a prayer that helps us withstand the attraction of keeping everything like it is: "Storm through this soul of mine; wake the sleeping parts of me; raise the dead parts of me; stand me on my feet, alert and praising in Your presence" (Eugene Peterson, *Living the Message* [San Francisco: Harper San Francisco, 1996], 99.)

To keep your leadership courageous, try praying these six short adventuresome prayers. These petitions will direct you to creative ways of doing ministry, shape you into Christlikeness, and demand your best efforts. These prayers could revolutionize your life:

1. Search me.
2. Break me.
3. Stretch me.
4. Lead me.
5. Use me.
6. Take me to the front lines.

A reluctance to risk, a fear of pioneer frontiers, or a refusal to retool ministry for these times shackles the work of God. In the long run, the seduction of safety strangles the life out of ministry and makes our efforts mediocre. More leaders with a do-or-die, break-out spirit are needed. Attempt great things for God.

Questions to Lower Fear of Risks at the New Frontiers

1. What is the worst thing that could happen?

2. What is the probability that the worst thing will happen?

3. What can I do to keep the worst from happening?

4. How can I lower the probabilities?

5. What are the possibilities if I take no risks?

6. What is the potential for achievement when I am willing to take a risk for a great cause?

Prayer for the Ephesians . . . and You

I pray that you,*
being rooted
and established in love,
may have the power,
together with all the saints,
to grasp how wide and long
and high and deep is the love of
Christ,
and to know this love
that surpasses knowledge—
that you* may be filled
to the measure
of all the fullness of God.

—The Apostle Paul
Eph. 3:17-19, NIV

---

*Put your name in these places to in-
crease impact of prayer.

TO KEEP SPIRITUALLY WELL, THE LEADER MUST GIVE CAREFUL ATTENTION TO INNER HEALTH.

11. SOLICIT PRAYER SUPPORT.

Stamina is strengthened when ministry is undergirded with prayer. Untapped prayer support is all around you. More than you think, people are interested in praying for you. You can have more prayer by asking for it. Think of all the people who would feel honored to take your needs to the throne of God. Here are possible sources of persons to pray for you:

✻ **People who nurtured your faith in the past.** Sunday School teachers, youth sponsors, former pastors, and friends from your home church will be delighted if you ask them to pray for you every day. And miles, clocks, or calendars cannot hinder the power of those prayers.

✻ **People you helped in crises.** Every individual or family you helped through a crisis is a prospective prayer supporter for your current ministry. Because of difficulties they shared with you, these people have a first-hand awareness of how much divine assistance is needed to serve others as you served them. They feel a bond with you because of the tender compassion you once showed them. That past experience creates an emotional/spiritual connection you can use to seek prayer support.

✳ People who need attention. Every congregation has individuals who desire more attention than a leader can give them. A common example is shut-ins who regret that they do not get more attention from the church. They may be frail or sick. Often they think they are unneeded because they cannot do what they once did in the church. Consequently, your request for prayer will focus them on concerns outside themselves, making them feel needed again. It involves them in an important ministry they can do and something you desperately need.

✳ People who serve with you. Christian workers experience magnificent enablement when they band together in prayer. Don't neglect prayer in your staff meetings, board meetings, and committee meetings.

Enlist members of your official decision-making group to promise to pray for each other and for you every day. Emphasize this request as being fully as significant as brilliant decisions or hard work. This togetherness in prayer develops a spiritual synergism.

✳ **Ministry peers share prayers.** One of the most significant inspirational thoughts I ever received in a letter are these words, "Let's trade prayers." Consider what an energetic enabling force for ministry those kinds of commitments create.

A Quote to Consider Again

Togetherness in

prayer develops a

spiritual synergism.

DON'T NEGLECT

PRAYER

IN YOUR

STAFF MEETINGS,

BOARD MEETINGS,

AND COMMITTEE

MEETINGS.

12. KINDLE A LOVE CONNECTION WITH SCRIPTURE.

Every pastor needs to sense the Bible coming alive, as if he or she were reading it for the first time. William H. Willimon sets a tone for such an exciting exploration: "You know enough about the Bible to know that the Bible is no mere rule book which will tell you or the church what to do on every possible subject. I think of the Bible more as a compass pointing us in the right direction than a road map telling us exactly which turn to take next."

Willimon continues, "The Bible doesn't answer all our questions; in fact, it may leave us with even more questions. But the Bible does put us in the proper frame of mind whereby we may learn to ask new questions and to be prepared for new and startling answers" (*With Glad and Generous Hearts* [Nashville: Upper Room Publishers, 1986], 85).

The Bible is filled with promises and ways to remedy many problems. Keep open to receive something invigorating from every passage. Try thinking of Scripture as

God's love letter that inspires your ministry.

Here are ways to increase your love for Scripture.

✳ Allow the Bible to shape you into Christlikeness. Saturate yourself with Scripture by attentive listening. Let personal encounters with Scripture impact details of your life. Enter into silent conversations with biblical characters, trying to reconstruct what they thought and felt during a particular biblical event.

Synchronize your thinking with the Bible's message so you hear, respond, and apply new truth to the current events of your life. Use Scripture to energize ministry.

✳ Stay receptive. Be open to wisdom and corrections concerning your own walk with God. Develop intimate friendship with the Author. Invest in quality time in the Bible. Carefully consider what the Spirit says from the printed page. Ask what the Father wants you to hear about your service to His people. What is the contemporary message for you in your spiritual journey?

✳ **Interrogate Scripture.** Ask questions of a passage. Walk around the meaning of a portion of Scripture. Check similar ideas in other biblical passages by using a concordance and commentaries. Probe the passage. Explore, research, study, compare, and contrast.

✳ **Personalize a passage.** Customize a promise by putting your name in it. What personal affirmation does a particular passage offer you?

A Quote to Consider Again

Synchronize your thinking with the Bible's message so you hear, respond, and apply new truth to the current events of your life.

TO BE A KINGDOM LEADER REQUIRES US TO SEE PEOPLE AS JESUS SEES THEM.

13. SEE PEOPLE AS JESUS DOES.

At first, this exercise seems simple. But too often we see people in light of what they can do for us or the institution. We see what service they can render, what they can give, or what impressions they can make.

Can you imagine Jesus saying, "You are a big catch, so I want you to be a part of My ministry because of all your wonderful skills, training, and prestige"?

Sometimes persons are labeled for the "trouble" they cause, for unwelcomed opinions they express, or for ways they muddle matters. In fact, some church leaders publicly advise people, "If you don't like what's happening here, move your membership to another church."

Can you imagine Jesus telling His disciples, "Get out of My way and stop complicating My plans"?

Doesn't Scripture say that Jesus saw people as sheep without a shepherd? As near as I can tell, genuine shepherds do not abandon or injure the sheep. To be a Kingdom leader requires us to see people as Jesus sees them. So we see them with problems and potential, with sins and possible saintliness, with brokenness and future wholeness.

The adventure of seeing people like Jesus saw them rings through these words from Pastor Eugene Peterson: "When we are in a community with those Christ loves and redeems, we are constantly finding out new things about them. They are new persons each morning, endless in their possibilities. We explore the fascinating depths of their friendship, share secrets of the quest. It is impossible to be bored in such a community, impossible to feel alienated among such people" (*Living the Message,* 20). It's time to say wow or amen.

The question of intentions must be factored into our notions about folks. H. G. Wells used a wonderfully enlightening phrase, "the secret splendor of our intentions." Concerning intentions, an old preacher in my youth loved to say, "Most of us want to be judged by our intentions while we evaluate others by their conduct." He is right. Then we were offered an effective remedy when the old preacher suggested, "We judge others by their intentions and allow them to judge us by our conduct."

A spiritual leader must remember a person may love art and not draw well, love music and not sing on pitch, or love carpentry and not be able to build a cabinet. Likewise, a church member may love God and still not serve efficiently or behave well. Charity for good intentions makes a church leader cultivate a heart of love toward everyone. He or she must believe God sees lofty motives behind many miserable mistakes. Thomas à Kempis once observed, "Man sees the deed but God sees the intention."

Likewise, a leader finds personal peace by leaving to God's judgment mixed or even impure motives that sometimes seem to lurk behind conduct. Motives, ours and theirs, are so complicated the Father reserves judgment for himself.

Seeing people as Jesus does impacts a minister's interior life and shows in his or her attitudes and speech. I remember being disappointed to hear a pastor remark, "So-and-so is trying to do me in, and I resent it." It is difficult to preach, serve sacraments, and pray when one allows himself or herself those responses. Let's realize "so-and-so" is not the one who is most hurt by our judgmental attitude.

The devotional writer Henri Nouwen puts these issues in perspective: "In our world of loneliness and despair, there is an enormous need for men and women who know the heart of God, a heart that forgives, that cares, that reaches out and wants to heal. In that heart there is no suspicion, no vindictiveness, no resentment, and not a tinge of hatred. It is a heart that wants only to give love and receive love in response" (*In the Name of Jesus* [New York: Crossroad, 1990], 24). That's the kind of leader I want to be.

Our Lord Wants Love to Show in Ministry

"My command is this:
Love each other as
I have loved you."
—Jesus
John 15:12, NIV

---

14. BE A PEACEMAKER.

Practice shalom. The Hebrew word *shalom* means to desire for another person everything he or she needs for contentment, freedom from trouble, and happy well-being.

Eugene Peterson clarifies the word's meaning: "*Shalom* gathers all aspects of wholeness that result from God's will being completed in us. . . . Every time Jesus healed, forgave, or called someone, we have a demonstration of *Shalom*" (*Living the Message,* 18).

There is another shade of meaning of *shalom* that richly resources right relationships. Of this idea Barclay wrote, "*Shalom* describes right personal relationships dealing with intimacy, fellowship, uninterrupted goodwill between persons" (*Daily Readings with William Barclay,* 78).

Closely tied to this idea is the amazing fact that every New Testament book speaks of peace—a close cousin to *shalom*. "Grace and peace" are found in all of Paul's Epistles, especially in the opening of his letters. And when Jesus leaves His disciples, He says, "Peace I leave with you; my peace I give to you" (John 14:27). Evidently peace is high on the agenda of the Kingdom.

Living *shalom* helps us benefit from the promise, "Blessed are the peacemakers: for they shall be called the children of God" (Matt. 5:9, KJV). To be called a child of God is among the highest titles anyone could have. Try emphasizing *shalom* in all your relationships inside and outside the church; it will revolutionize your world and your perspective.

If peacemaking seems too difficult, be assured that our Savior never requires anything that He does not empower us to do by the Spirit. At the same time, fulfilling our Lord's directives makes us better leaders and gives us inner satisfaction.

A Quote to Consider Again

Evidently peace is high on the agenda of the Kingdom.

Case Study— Joe's Reality Check

An exercise called "Reality Check" shook Joe Van Buren at a leaders' conference. Each person was asked to draw a 12-space grid representing the previous 12 hours. Then they were asked to write one word for each hour representing the major event.

Joe felt bothered by the questions that followed:

1. Did you say anything during these time frames that you knew was false?

2. Did you exaggerate or stretch truth?

3. Did you withhold acceptance because of a false assumption?

Consider what the exercise means. What is the lesson for Joe and for us?

CONDITIONING

15. TEST YOUR OPINIONS AND CONCLUSIONS.

Just as clocks verify time and calendars verify dates, leaders need fair-minded people to verify their actions and check their attitudes. It is easy to fool ourselves.

Though it may sometimes shock us, our conclusions are not always accurate. Adding two and two, we sometimes get five, or even nine. Some church leaders live in a continuous emotional stew because they believe others do not want to be loyal, loving, and effective. Some even think parishioners will stop giving if the church has money in the bank. False assumptions, unfounded presuppositions, and inaccurate conclusions can happen to any of us. How can we test our perspectives?

Think of the stereotypes so many of us carry in our heads. Here's a sample list of what you sometimes hear around the church:

a. Denominational and parachurch CEOs don't care about little people.

b. The rich are always stingy.

c. Educated people are pompous.

d. Big churches aren't spiritual.
e. Poor people are lazy.
f. Southerners are more friendly than Westerners.
g. Young people are not serious about following God.
h. All golden-agers are against change.
i. Laypeople are apathetic.
j. Strong people can't be trusted.

Make your own list to help identify how inaccurate your presuppositions may be. It's amazing how we kid ourselves about serious matters.

One pastor believes his congregation is spiritual because it doesn't grow; his presupposition says, "Growing churches compromise the truth."

Another church leader believes his church wins 50 converts each year because of their modern worship practices; the reality—new people come because of a vigorous personal evangelism ministry led by a lay leader.

Still another minister thinks his church is friendly because members are cordial to each other; the reality—visitors feel left out because this congregation is so busy fellow-shipping with itself.

To make an even closer application to soul conditioning, one leader thinks a half hour per day in devotional exercises makes him spiritually sturdy. But something is wrong because his church members say to each other, "We expected him to be our pastor, but we have to pastor him because his homelife is so stagnant."

Leaders need to intentionally design strategies to test their perspectives. They need feedback. They need to listen closely to people who will share differences of opinion. The higher one's position in an organization, the less likely people are to level with him or her. Usually individuals are less candid with a bishop than with a janitor.

It is the frightening nature of leadership that one can operate according to outrageous assumptions. Some leaders fool themselves for years. Others make less important though mistaken assumptions: everyone chuckled when a new pastor assumed all members of his church's decision group belonged to one political party when half were registered in another party.

One checks the validity of suppositions by careful listening. Elspeth Huxley's novel *The Flaming Trees of Thika* offers a plan that might work for a church leader: "The best way to find things out is not to ask questions at all. If you fire off a question, it is like firing off a gun—bang it goes, and everything takes flight and runs for shelter. But if you sit quite still and pretend not to be looking, all the little facts will come and peck around your feet, situations will venture forth from thickets, and intentions will creep out and sun themselves on a stone; and if you are very patient, you will see and understand a great deal more than a man with a gun does" (quoted in *Vital Speeches of the Day,* 1997, 189).

Check what you teach/preach against Scripture. Question yourself to see if your conclusions are charitable. Keep reminding yourself that you hold a sacred trust from God and from those you lead.

16. *THINK LIKE A PHILIPPIAN.*

The apostle Paul offered "how to think" instructions to his sweetheart church at Philippi. To think like a Philippian, the servant leader intentionally puts Phil. 4:8-9 into practice. Consider the compelling contemporary way *The Message* states Paul's directive: "Summing it all up, friends, I'd say you'll do best by filling your minds and meditating on things true, noble, reputable, authentic, compelling, gracious—the best, not the worst; the beautiful, not the ugly; things to praise, not things to curse. Put into practice what you learned from me, what you heard and saw and realized. Do that, and God, who makes everything work together, will work you into his most excellent harmonies."

Ponder that passage. Enjoy its harmonies and melodies. Such positive, lofty, noble thoughts shape our lives. The more you think about God's grace, the more loving you become. The more your thoughts dwell on the goodness of Christian people, the richer your life becomes. Conversely, the more you think about grievances, the more you see them. Then you miss the glories of goodness and the surprises of generosity.

It is an inescapable axiom of life and ministry—whatever fills your mind will be magnified in your life.

There are few difficulties encountered by the spiritual leader that cannot be overcome with the power of prayer and a persistent faith. Solutions often begin with Philippian thinking.

A Quote to Consider Again

**Some leaders
fool themselves
into
believing a lie
for years.**

Case Study— Tim's More-than- Positive Attitude

For years, some preachers have joked about the power of negative thinking. Others have seriously wondered how they could think positively about their assignment and its limitations.

Recently Tim read Phil. 4:8-9, and it affected him as if he were reading it for the first time. He made a list of Paul's advices on a Post-it Note and stuck the note on the telephone in his study. For a month, every time someone phoned, he made it a practice to consider the main message of the call against Paul's instructions for healthy thinking. After a month, he began thinking like a Philippian.

Write your own list.

17. FOCUS ON ESSENTIALS.

Losing focus is a common occurrence for leaders. But since a church's business is to enable people to grow spiritually, the main thing must be the main thing. This becomes reality by making the Great Commission operational.

As you remember from your experiences with the Bible, the Great Commission has two simple but profound dimensions: (1) win people to Christ and (2) teach people how to live a Christ-saturated life by bringing everything under the Lordship of Christ.

The church landscape is strewn with congregations that embraced many good things while neglecting the first thing. The test of an accurate focus is whether an attitude, activity, or achievement is controlled by the two parts of the Great Commission—one is not enough. This refocusing works most effectively when we ask ourselves and our Savior whether the direction of our ministry is pleasing to Him.

Without a thorough commitment to a crystal clear focus, churches and pastors may be attracted or pressured into doing many good things that take the church away from its main mission. Not knowing what to do, they do everything or they do nothing.

Though many factors may cause a loss of focus, at least five concerns should be considered:

❋ **Circumstances.** Often leaders lose focus when difficult circumstances arise. Then the predictable question pops up, "Why me?" One old saint heard a younger believer ask that question and answered, "Why not you?"

Disease, disappointment, and death are human experiences for believers as well as nonbelievers. Giving thoughtful attention to who is with us in trying situations helps maintain focus.

❋ **Discounting positives.** Though the phrase comes from Psychologist David Burn (*USA Today,* August 18, 1997, 43), it describes a leader who discounts positive experiences and refuses to accept joyous events. They falsely reason something bad will happen soon or they feel unworthy of blessings. Examples are self-talk like this: "I have a good marriage but it can't last because I am such a loser." Or "For five years our family hasn't had a serious illness, so it's time for something bad to happen."

✳ **Mistaken judgments.** Overgeneralizations sometimes fog our focus. False conclusions debilitate our focus when they cause us to exaggerate misunderstandings or make us spend too much time on a mistake we made. Another example happens when we accept as fact some negative emotion we feel about a person or event.

✳ **Troubled people.** No pastor should allow mean-spirited people to bruise or cripple his or her soul. Many churches have at least one person who wants control. Sometimes this person will do anything to be in charge. Sometimes he or she causes a congregation to mistrust or mistreat leaders. Though in Western society the majority rules, too much credence is sometimes given to one or two troubled persons in the church. We enjoy saying, "The squeaky wheel gets the grease."

Conversely, to keep accurately focused on Kingdom priorities, a leader must listen to all sides. The Christ-centered leader cultivates harmony and seeks to implement the mind of Christ. To be a well-informed leader, it should be realized that persons in the minority sometimes have worthwhile perspectives that need to be heard and heeded. But on average, one troubled person in a church or a nagging voice from a leader's past should not determine congregational priorities.

✳ **Paranoia.** We enjoy a good laugh about a secular boss who asked, "Who said I was paranoid? What are their names? And why are they chasing me all the time?"

Let's underscore a fact of ministry. Sheep are unpredictable and prone to wander. According to an engaging writer from out of the past, the primary purpose of sheep is to complicate the life of their shepherd. From the same author I read, "Without sheep, the world would have no need for shepherds."

Let's stamp out leadership paranoia. Often when parishioners behave like sheep, they do not intend to hurt a shepherd. Many congregational problems are nothing more than a leader making a big deal over sheep acting like sheep. Whenever human beings get together in a group, we should expect to have some human problems. This being true, leaders should rethink their sniffling self-pity about problem church members.

A paranoia easily infects leaders when they mistakenly conclude anyone who does not agree with their program, performance, or proclamation is an enemy. Reading about ministry paranoia sounds childish, but it oftentimes blindsides even experienced leaders. Seek to live liberated from feeling victimized by the people God has called you to serve.

Consider this true story from my pilgrimage. I know a congregation where most church services highlighted the devil's power or openly suspected every congregant's commitment to Christ. Sometimes both of these negative themes showed up in the same sermon.

With snow-white intentions, one spiritually mature woman suggested to the minister that the people needed more hope, victory, faith, and a lot more grace. The pastor overreacted and scolded this lady in the foyer. He preached condescending correctives from the pulpit. He complained to the district superintendent and anyone else who would listen. And though the pastor did not intend for it to happen, he subverted the congregation's confidence in the one who made the suggestion even as he made many think he was spiritually immature.

In a few years the leader moved to another assignment, yet the veteran believer suffered embarrassment for years and was muzzled for life.

Years passed. The pastor is wiser now and nearing retirement. The person who offered the suggestion has been in heaven for a decade. But in moments of musing, the minister wishes he could tell the old saint how right she was. After all the years, the pastor realizes he turned a potential spiritual booster into a pseudoenemy. Now he realizes he impoverished them both.

Be warned. Personal paranoia is contagious, ruinous, and generally mistaken.

Like feathers scattered in Aesop's fable, many consequences of paranoia can never be recovered and repaired.

Spiritual Exercises

What Fogs Focus?

In Section 17, the following list of attitudes and practices that cause leaders to lose focus are discussed. Which apply to you?

✦ Difficult circumstances

✦ Discounting positives

✦ Mistaken judgments

✦ Troubled people

✦ Pastoral paranoia

Add your own issues to the list. Often a foggy focus is an inside job—inside our mind and spirit.

How can one keep focused for a lifetime of Christian service?

18. DISCOVER SATISFACTION IN SERVICE.

Service stands at the heart of Christianity. Doing good to the souls and bodies of human beings is the most tangible way we express love to our Savior.

Consider these two true parables from Greg Anderson's book *Living Life on Purpose*.

A great-grandson of slaves, Robert Brown grew up in Highpoint, North Carolina. His grandmother, a Christian woman who matched her words with actions, raised him in her home. Once when they had barely enough food for their family, Robert questioned his grandmother about her giving food away. After motioning her grandson to sit beside her, she replied, "If I never teach you anything else, remember that what you got is not your own. It belongs to the Lord, and the Lord wants us to share it with others" ([San Francisco: Harper, 1997], 51). Service is the honest acknowledgment that everything belongs to God. All we have and are is loaned us to be used as channels of grace and instruments of spiritual transformation.

A second story from Anderson shines a blazing light in the dark places where leaders are tempted to feel sorry for themselves. Alice Gaither, customer service director for a large telecommunications corporation, good-naturedly refers to herself as "the flak catcher." She explains how she copes, even finding satisfaction in her stress-producing job: "I can handle any complaint as long as I keep the mental discipline to understand that it is an opportunity to serve" (52). For ministry, maybe such mental discipline should be understood to come from supernatural enablement. Doing good to others provides incredible satisfaction for the one who serves.

Service has many expressions, forms, and locations—as many as there are people who need us. Ways of serving are as varied as those who serve. Scripture is filled with service examples, such as a cup of cold water, an affirming word, a healing prayer, or a meal and hospitality—as Jesus enjoyed at the home of Lazarus.

Service is something helpful and beautiful we do for another in the name of Jesus.

Longfellow's sentence explains, "The life of a man consists not in seeing visions and in dreaming dreams, but in active love and in willing service" (Ted Goodman, ed., *The Forbes Book of Business Quotations* [New York: Black Dog and Leventhal Publishers, 1997], 763).

Service has three well-defined outcomes. Service (1) benefits the receiver, such as the student, the sick, the homeless, the hungry; (2) pleases God—in serving people we serve God; Jesus explained, "Inasmuch as ye have done it unto one of the least of these my brethren, ye have done it unto me" (KJV); and (3) blesses the one who serves.

Former government leader John W. Gardner wisely observes, "When people are serving, life is no longer meaningless" (*Forbes Book of Business Quotations,* 763). Give careful consideration to this third dimension because it offers such enormous potential for building a satisfying faith. It starts as leaders move their motivation from duty to delight. Just as a good marriage is a gift one gives to himself or herself, service is a gift we give ourselves. As Gary Morsch and Dean Nelson explain in *Heart and Soul,* "When people see that being involved in the needs of others is part of their purpose for existing, they can't forget it" ([Kansas City: Beacon Hill Press of Kansas City, 1997], 107). Once such satisfaction is discovered, the servant starts searching for new ways to serve and new ways to receive satisfaction from serving.

For service to make maximum impact on giver and receiver, it must be energized by love. This love dimension motivates ministers to follow the serving examples of their Lord. That's what drove Mother Teresa to make a difference on Calcutta's streets. That's what inspires President Jimmy Carter to commit time to Habitat for Humanity.

Service is a talented teacher giving 30 years to an inner-city school where few others were willing to stay. Service is a well-established pastor starting a church among immigrants with little support and few people. Service is what you do for the sheer joy of helping someone in Jesus' name.

Three surprises come as we serve.

CONDITIONING

As an unexpected bonus from God, we discover with Henri Nouwen, "It is safe to be weak because we are surrounded by a creative strength" (Henri Nouwen, *Intimacy* [San Francisco: Harper and Row, 1969], 36). Service connects us to creative strength.

Another rich reward comes when we hear C. S. Lewis connect service satisfaction with a call to ministry: "I believe that the men of this age think too much about the state of nations and the situation of the world . . . In the poor man who knocks at my door, in my ailing mother, in the young man who seeks my advice, the Lord himself is present: therefore let us wash His feet" (*The Quotable C. S. Lewis* [Wheaton, Ill.: Tyndale, 1993], 534). Service, satisfaction, compassion, grace, fulfillment, love, and God's approval are all wonderfully inter-twined in our efforts to help another in the name of Jesus.

The third benefit is freedom from the manacles of selfishness. British cynic Cyril Connolly was right: "We are all serving a life sentence in the dungeon of self" (as quoted in Herb Miller, *Connecting with God* [Nashville: Abingdon, 1994], 98). Service frees us from this solitary confinement because it forces us to consider the needs of others. Like other areas of happy living, the more we give the less we think about ourselves.

Sadly, too many churches are loveless, dreary places where congregants meet out of duty, habit, and tradition. In those congregations, officials go about their work without thinking much about how they might infuse service with love, which always draws people to Christ.

Try tripling love for people you serve and see how much more fun you have being a leader. Every responsibility goes better with love. Check your satisfaction for service against your love for God, love for the people, and love for your ministry.

Love can be used over and over again as a way to get back on track. Edward J. Lavin tells the story of a high school in the eastern part of the United States that exempts students the last half of their senior year so they can devote themselves to some form of service. As a result, high school seniors work in hospitals, clinics, schools, and nursing homes. The faculty regularly see enormous changes in students as they become more mature, more sure of themselves, and more enriched. Lavin offers this powerfully true summary sentence, "The act of service pulls us out of ourselves, generates in us the power of charity and love, and perhaps most important of all, makes us feel good about ourselves" (*Life Meditations* [New York: Wings Books, 1993], n.p.). Lavin's statement is true for any spiritual leader who purposefully saturates his or her service with satisfaction.

Spiritual Exercise

Try tripling love for people you serve and see how much more fun you have being a leader.

19. PRACTICE THE PRESENCE.

The idea, of course, comes from Brother Lawrence, the 16th-century monk. He discovered God could be as present in the kitchen while he washed greasy pots and pans for the monastery as He was present in communion in the sanctuary.

Firmly rooted in the biblical teaching of our Father's omnipresence, practicing the presence means God is everywhere present all the time. Carried to its logical conclusion, God is as near me in my car traveling to a pastoral responsibility as He is present when I preach or teach. I need only recognize Him to enjoy the presence.

Thus strength for details of ministry comes when we welcome the always present God. It means we can see Him in creation, relationships, victories, and problems too.

A spiritually charming woman used to serve at a small Kansas City restaurant. I loved to eat there because she radiated the spirit of Jesus. And she celebrated His closeness by a well-placed word to customers, like "I am going to take my vacation in California next week, if God wills." Or when customers would tell of a pleasant event, she might say, "I know you thanked the Lord, didn't you?"

Why not sing and practice the words of the chorus, "He's as near as the mention of His name"?

Stop and Stretch Your Soul

"Let any person (pastor/leader) turn to God in earnest, let him begin to exercise himself unto godliness, let him seek to develop his powers of spiritual receptivity by trust and obedience and humility, and the results will exceed anything he may have hoped in his leaner and weaker days."

A. W. Tozer

20. ENJOY GOD.

For some hard-to-explain reason, some believers dread being alone with God. Perhaps they are afraid because their mental picture of God is as an authoritative judge, accusing parent, perfectionistic professor, absentee landlord, or unbending boss. Thus their contacts with God may seem uncomfortable. Obviously, the problem is with them rather than with God.

The remedy is to always remember that God is for you and with you. Much more than even the best human parent, God wants you to enjoy adventures in Christian service. He wants you to grow a sturdy soul, and He stands ready to help you do it.

A little while ago, I heard a pastor tell about an early morning appointment he kept with God. Being a night person, he has difficulty getting up in the morning. After dragging himself out to pray on a particular morning, with sleepy eyes and a sluggish brain, he decided to go back to bed. Then he experienced an inner impression as real as an audible voice: "So you would rather sleep than keep your appointment with

Me?" God's friendly chastisement was a first step in transforming that leader's duty-motivated devotional life into winsome fellowship with the Father.

Rejoice. Ministry by definition makes you a partner with Omnipotence. Though you will always be a junior partner, you are a significant participant in the work God is doing in His world.

When you consider your many tender associations with the Father, you can cherish what others fear. Rejoice because God is the . . .

> JUDGE who sets you free when you deserve imprisonment or death.
>
> PARENT who affirms you as a member of the family of God on earth and in heaven.
>
> PROFESSOR who teaches you truth about yourself and the world.
>
> PROVIDER who supplies shelter, security, and warmth.
>
> LORD—Jesus is the Lord (the Boss) of your life.

What others fear about God can be the very things you cherish.

Though the concept of enjoying God is deeply rooted in Scripture, the Westminster Catechism states it in beautiful shorthand language when it asks, "What is the chief end of humankind?" Then the Catechism answers with six words that sound like a heavenly praise symphony, "To glorify God and *enjoy Him forever.*"

Look for imaginative ways to enjoy God. Discover gladness, fascination, and exhilaration in prayer, Scripture reading, and hymns. Sturdy souls have learned how to enjoy the sparkle and satisfaction of friendship with God's people.

Why not do yourself a favor? Cultivate a sense of adventuresome ministry for the sheer joy of it. Remove the glum for a week and it might never come back. The time has come for every Christian leader to build into the fabric of Kingdom service an enjoyable friendship with God.

Friendship with God links us with His nearby grace—so we are never alone in any assignment He gives us.

Review

1. Commit to personal soul care
2. Cherish simple abundance
3. Learn to love people
4. Use convenient resources
5. Celebrate your calling as more than a profession
6. Apply your preaching to yourself
7. Retain intimacy with God
8. Purposefully seek direction for ministry
9. Cultivate a soul friend
10. Pioneer new frontiers
11. Solicit prayer support
12. Kindle a love connection with Scripture
13. See people as Jesus does
14. Be a peacemaker
15. Test your opinions and conclusions
16. Think like a Philippian
17. Focus on essentials
18. Discover satisfaction in service
19. Practice the presence
20. Enjoy God

Cherish Your
Magnificent Privileges

By growing a great sturdy soul, you can rediscover supernatural energy and creative strength in every expression of your ministry. Stretch your soul. Demonstrate the love of Christ in every level of your living. Then the work of God under your care will flourish. Then you will experience adventures in preaching, a holy presence in care of souls, awe in leading worship, and direction in administration.

Cherish these facts: God wants your ministry to profoundly impact those you serve. But He has even more planned for you. While serving others, your Father wants to shape you into Christlikeness. Beyond your fondest dreams, He wants to add amazing adventure to your ministry.

Think of your privileges: Service for Christ takes you places you would never go without Him. Ministry allows you to impact people you otherwise would never know. And partnership with God permits you to receive grace and experience personal growth.

Genuine greatness, the kind Jesus promised, enriches your purpose for living and increases your passion for Christ. Growing your soul blasts corrosion away that eats at your vision.

A thousand leaders intentionally growing sturdy souls could easily light gospel fires of hope, revival, devotion, conviction, servanthood, imagination, creativity, and holy living across the entire world. Why not be one of them?

Now a Personal Word

Let me borrow John's words to Gaius to tell you how much pastors and their work mean to me. "How truly I love you! We're the best of friends, and I pray for good fortune in everything you do, and for your good health—that your everyday affairs prosper, as well as your soul!" (3 John 1-2, TM).

Straight ahead for Christ.
—NBW